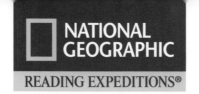

W9-CHA-238

WILDLIFE RESCUE

Dolphin Rescue

By Glen Phelan
Illustrated by Dan Burr

PICTURE CREDITS

3 (top & bottom left), 3 (bottom right), 4 (top & bottom left), 4 (top right), 5 (bottom right), 44 (top & bottom left), 44 (top right), 45 (bottom right), 46 (bottom left), 47 (top right & bottom left), 48 (top & bottom left), 48 (bottom left & right) Getty Images; 5 (bottom left), 45 (bottom left), 46 Corbis; 44 Mapping Specialists, Ltd.; 45 © Charlie Phillips/SplashdownDirect.com; 48 © The Image Bank/Getty Images.

PUBLISHED BY THE NATIONAL GEOGRAPHIC SOCIETY

Produced through the worldwide resources of the National Geographic Society, John M. Fahey, Jr., President and Chief Executive Officer; Gilbert M. Grosvenor, Chairman of the Board.

PREPARED BY NATIONAL GEOGRAPHIC SCHOOL PUBLISHING

Sheron Long, Chief Executive Officer; Samuel Gesumaria, President; Francis Downey, Vice President and Publisher; Richard Easby, Editorial Manager; Anne M. Stone, Editor; Margaret Sidlosky, Director of Design and Illustrations; Jim Hiscott, Design Manager; Cynthia Olson, Ruth Ann Thompson, Art Directors; Matt Wascavage, Director of Publishing Services; Lisa Pergolizzi, Production Manager.

MANUFACTURING AND QUALITY CONTROL

Christopher A. Liedel, Chief Financial Officer; Phillip L. Schlosser, Vice President; Clifton M. Brown III, Director.

CONSULTANT

Mary Anne Wengel

BOOK DESIGN

Steve Curtis Design, Inc.

Published by the National Geographic Society
1145 17th Street N.W.
Washington, D.C. 20036-4688

Product #4U1005102
ISBN: 978-1-4263-5095-5

Printed in Mexico.

17 16 15 14 13 12
10 9 8 7 6 5 4 3 2

Contents

The Characters

Wildlife Rescue is a company that helps wild animals. They take care of animals that are sick, injured, or in danger. When the animals are ready, Wildlife Rescue returns them to the wild. This is never an easy task. Each rescue becomes an adventure. It takes our group of heroes all over the country. From the forests of the Northeast to the shores of the West Coast, Wildlife Rescue is ready to roll.

Victor Montoya is an animal expert at the County Zoo. He is also part of the Wildlife Rescue team that travels the country helping wildlife in trouble.

Susan Montoya is a veterinarian (an animal doctor). She treats injured and sick animals at the County Zoo. As a member of the Wildlife Rescue team, Dr. Montoya treats animals in the wild.

Angela Montoya is 11 years old. She hopes to be a vet like her mom. Angie likes to travel with her parents when they go on wildlife rescue missions.

Jonathan Montoya is Angie's nine year-old brother. He asks a million questions because he always wants to learn more about animals.

Jason Tenbrook works for the United States Forest Service. He is a wildlife biologist and studies how animals behave. Jason also takes care of wounded animals until they can be released back into the wild.

CHAPTER 1

A Close Encounter

Jonathan tapped his hand on the surface of the water. The water was chilly, but that didn't matter. He was too excited. He tapped again. A moment later a silvery shadow swam into view just below the surface. It glided right past him. He quickly turned one way, then the other. Where did it go?

Jonathan felt something nudge his hand. It startled him.

"Huh?" He jerked his hand back.

Suddenly Jonathan was face-to-face with an 8-foot, 400-pound, silver and white bottlenose dolphin.

"Jonathan, say hello to Half Moon," said biologist Natalie Murtoff.

"Hi there."

Half Moon dropped her head and floated alongside Jonathan. He stroked the dolphin's side with his hand. He was unsure at first, barely touching the dolphin with his fingertips.

"Don't be shy," Natalie urged. "Just stay away from her face and the **blowhole** on top of her head. Those are sensitive spots and we don't want to hurt her."

---

blowhole – a nostril in the top of the head of a dolphin. The blowhole is used to breathe

Jonathan stroked the dolphin's side with the palm of his hand. Her skin was as smooth as silk.

"Can I try?" asked his sister Angela, who was floating ten feet away.

"Sure. Just tap your hand on the water," said Natalie.

Angela tapped, and Half Moon swam toward her. She could tell that Half Moon was very strong by how quickly the large animal moved in the water. Yet, Angela felt very safe.

"She's so gentle."

Natalie agreed. "Dolphins usually are, especially around children. I think they sense that children are not going to hurt them."

As Angela petted Half Moon's smooth skin, she felt something bumpy near her belly.

"What's this? It looks like a scar. It's shaped like a C."

"It could be a C, but it reminds me of a half moon," said Natalie.

"Half moon? Is that how she got her name?"

"Yep."

Angela was curious. "What happened? Did she cut herself on a sharp rock?"

"Maybe, or it could be from a shark attack."

Jonathan's eyes widened. "Sharks? Cool!"

"Sharks and killer whales are about the only enemies dolphins have, besides humans. A shark might have rammed her with its snout. Or it might have scraped her with its teeth. Dolphins can hold their own, though, even against a hungry shark. See that long beak?"

Natalie pointed to the dolphin's long, rounded snout.

"That beak really packs a punch when a dolphin rams it into a shark's side. And dolphins usually travel in groups called pods. They protect one another. So Half Moon and a few other dolphins can easily chase a shark away."

As Natalie finished speaking, Half Moon slowly slipped away from the children's hands. She started swimming toward shore.

"Oh no, is she leaving?" Angela asked.

"No, she wants you to swim with her," said Natalie. "That's why she's moving slowly.

C'mon, let's go."

Delighted, Angela and Jonathan swam next to Half Moon. Now and then, they reached out to pet their new swimming buddy. Angela couldn't help but giggle.

"Hey, Jon. We're swimming with a dolphin. How cool is that?"

It was pretty cool. But then Angela and Jonathan Montoya got to do a lot of cool stuff. Their mother, Dr. Susan Montoya, was a veterinarian at a zoo in Missouri. Their father,

Victor, was an animal trainer at the zoo. Angela and Jonathan spent a lot of time there. They helped the zookeepers care for the animals.

Besides their regular jobs, the Montoyas and their friend Jason Tenbrook ran a company called Wildlife Rescue. They helped wild animals that were sick, hurt, or in danger. Their adventures took them all over the country. Angela and Jonathan went along whenever they could—when it didn't interfere with school or soccer.

Today they were on the coast of Southern Oregon at a research center for **marine mammals.** Here, scientists study dolphins and whales that live in the cool waters off the coast. The scientists at the center had invited Wildlife Rescue to learn more about these animals. Susan and Victor worked with the dolphins at their zoo. However, there's a big difference between caring for an animal in a zoo and rescuing it in the wild. So they jumped at the chance to learn how to rescue dolphins and other mammals that live in the ocean.

marine mammals – mammals that live in the ocean

Angela and Jonathan were learning about these animals too. For the most part, though, this week was going to be one of swimming and fun. It was off to a great start.

"Hey, let's swim over to Mom and Dad," said Jonathan.

Their parents stood in waist-deep water with Jason about a hundred yards away. Two scientists from the research center were showing them the proper way to move a dolphin. Suddenly one of the scientists looked toward them and started waving his hands. He was yelling something. They stopped swimming so they could hear.

". . . Call . . . in . . . got a call . . . We got a call. Come on in."

"Uh-oh. Time to go kids." Natalie clapped her hands to get Half Moon's attention. Then she swept her hand toward the open waters. Half Moon understood the signal and swam away. Angela and Jonathan waved goodbye.

"Okay kids, let's swim to shore. Your vacation is about to get a lot more exciting."

CHAPTER 2

Stranded

Five minutes later, Angela, Jonathan, and Natalie stepped out of the surf and onto the beach. Jonathan ran up to his parents.

"Mom, Dad, did you see us swimming with Half Moon? It was awesome!"

"I'll bet it was," replied Susan Montoya. She wrapped a towel around his shoulders.

Their dad tossed a towel to Angela. "No time to change your clothes, kids. Grab your flip-flops and jump in the truck."

"What happened?" Natalie asked her co-worker, Paul Orzo.

"We got a call from the police. A dolphin is **stranded** on the banks of the Coos River. We will have to hurry."

---

stranded – to place or leave in a helpless or difficult position

The Wildlife Rescue truck followed the research center van. They drove on Highway 101 along the coast of the Pacific Ocean. The water sparkled like jewels in the late afternoon sun.

Angela pulled a T-shirt over her wet suit. "So how did the dolphin get stranded?"

"We're not sure," answered Jason. "The storm last night might have had something to do with it. Strong waves could have pushed the dolphin toward the river where it flows into the ocean."

"Then the dolphin swam up the river by mistake?" guessed Angela.

"Possibly. Although dolphins sometimes swim into rivers on purpose."

"But how did it end up on the riverbank?"

"Maybe it was chasing a fish," Jonathan mumbled as he picked sand from between his toes.

"Don't be ridiculous, Jon," scolded Angela.

"Actually, your brother may be right," said their mom.

Jonathan smugly said, "I told you so," even though it had been a wild guess.

"Dolphins are fast, powerful swimmers," continued their mom. "Sometimes a dolphin swims so fast that it jumps out of the water as it snags a fish. If it's close to shore, it might end up on a beach or a riverbank. That's just one way dolphins get stranded. Scientists don't always know why."

"Can it wiggle back to the water?" asked Angela.

"Not if it's out all the way. If it isn't rescued, it will probably die."

Now Angela was worried.

Fifteen minutes later they pulled off the highway. Another road took them along the river. Soon they saw two police cars parked near the riverbank. The van backed up to the spot where the police officers stood. Doors opened and everyone sprang into action.

The dolphin lay on the sandy bank. Only its tail touched the water. Paul Orzo and Susan Montoya examined the dolphin. They were both veterinarians. Dr. Montoya took a blood sample from the tail. She would examine it later to tell if

the dolphin was sick. Other rescuers put plastic
bags of ice around the fins of the dolphin. The
ice would keep the dolphin cool on this hot day.
An overheated dolphin could die.

Angela and Jonathan helped hold the ice on
the dolphin. Natalie said it was a male.

"He looks like Half Moon," noted Jonathan.

"Except for all these marks," added Angela.

This bottlenose dolphin had many scars and

scratches on its body. Angela and Jonathan
wondered if he got banged up in the storm.

"Okay, let's get him in the van," said one of
the scientists. Angela and Jonathan stepped
back. The adults gently lifted the large mammal
onto a stretcher. Two of the police officers
helped carry the stretcher into the van.

The van had special equipment to help
marine mammals. In fact, it was more like a

dolphin ambulance. Inside was a large tank of water. The stretcher fit inside the tank so that half of the dolphin was below water. Jonathan thought it looked like the dolphin was taking a bath.

"Will he be all right?" Angela asked.

Natalie could see how concerned she was. "We can't find anything wrong with him, but we don't know for sure. Do you want to ride in the van back to the research center? You and Jonathan can help keep him cool."

That sounded terrific. Natalie showed them how to use sponges to squeeze the cool water on the dolphin. She and Dr. Montoya rode with the kids to keep an eye on the patient.

"Hey, look at that!" Jonathan pointed out the back window of the van as they pulled away. Out in the river, a dolphin leaped out of the water. Then it dove out of sight. Had it been watching the whole time? Was it the stranded dolphin's mate? Did it know that someone was helping? Angela and Jonathan wondered. So did the scientists.

CHAPTER 3

Dolphins to the Rescue

Paul and Susan had some good news. The stranded dolphin, which they called Sandy, was not sick after all.

"However," said Paul, "he is very nervous."

"Dolphins get nervous?" asked Jonathan. "How can you tell?"

"Well for starters, they talk a lot. That's what Sandy's doing."

"Dolphins talk?" Angela couldn't believe it.

Paul laughed. "Oh, not like you and me. They make clicks, whistles, barks, and other sounds." Paul turned to Susan. "Sandy is also swimming strangely. Darting off in different directions."

They watched Sandy swimming in a lagoon, a small lake that was connected to the bay. A gate closed off the lagoon from the bay. The scientists could easily watch the dolphin in the lagoon. When they were sure he was well enough, the gate would be opened and the dolphin would be free.

"Maybe something's wrong with his echolocation," suggested Susan.

"His what?" asked Jonathan.

"Echolocation. It's a way that dolphins find things underwater. Dolphins make clicking sounds that are too high-pitched for humans to hear. These sounds travel through the water, bounce off objects, and return to the dolphin."

"Oh, like an echo," said Jonathan.

"Exactly. Dolphins can tell where objects are by how long it takes a sound to return to them. That comes in handy in murky or deep waters where there's not enough light to see well."

"Sandy's echolocation is probably fine, though," said Paul. "I think he's just acting strange because he's in a small space. If he has no other problems, we'll release him tomorrow."

"Good, then he can get back with the other fish," said Jonathan.

Angela caught his mistake immediately. "A dolphin isn't a fish, Jon. It's a mammal."

"Whatever," Jonathan shrugged.

"It's an important difference," Susan pointed out. "Like most other mammals, dolphins don't lay eggs. Instead, they give birth to their young. Then they nurse their young with milk. And they breathe air, like us."

"That's what the blowhole is for, right?" asked Angela.

"Right. The blowhole is like a nostril, for breathing. The dolphin usually comes to the surface two or three times a minute to take a breath. On deep dives, though, it can go seven or eight minutes between breaths."

Jonathan wondered, "Why is it on top of the head instead of on its nose?"

"That's a great question," said Paul. "Watch how Sandy swims on the surface of the water. The blowhole is open to the air even though his face is in the water. So he can swim and keep an eye on things while he's breathing."

"It's like snorkeling," said Angela.

That reminded Susan. She looked at her watch. "We have to go, kids. We're supposed to meet Dad and Uncle Jason for snorkeling."

An hour later Jason and the Montoyas were exploring the cool, clear waters off the coast.

"Hey Angie! Did you see all those blue and yellow fish by the shipwreck?"

Jonathan put his head back down in the water. Through his face mask he could view the watery world below.

They were snorkeling in a calm area of the bay. The water was about 20 feet deep here.

Below them were the remains of a fishing boat that had sunk years ago. The colorful fish were an added attraction.

"Don't drift too far from the boat," their mom called out. She, Victor, and Jason were also in the water. Natalie stayed on the boat that brought them there.

Suddenly something caught Victor's eye. He pointed. "What's that?"

It was a fin cutting through the water about 30 feet away!

Susan pointed in the opposite direction. "There's another one. And another over there! Jason, watch out!"

The fin passed within a few feet of Jason. He twirled quickly to catch a glance.

Angela and Jonathan looked up and saw the fins. "Are they sharks?" Angela yelled out nervously.

Natalie had a good view from the boat. "No, they're . . ."

Before she could finish, one of the animals leaped into the air.

"Dolphins!" Jonathan yelled gleefully.

Everyone breathed a sigh of relief. Natalie counted five fins. One by one, the dolphins broke water in graceful arches. They began to circle the swimmers.

"Looks like you'll get another chance to swim with the dolphins," Victor told his children.

Something was odd, Natalie thought. The circle was getting smaller and smaller. It was almost like the dolphins were trying to herd the swimmers together. Suddenly she saw why.

Another fin poked through the water about 50 feet away. Natalie knew it wasn't a dolphin this time. It headed straight for the swimmers.

Natalie cupped her hands to her mouth. "Shark in the water! Stay together!"

They all looked where Natalie was pointing. As the shark approached the circle of dolphins, it changed direction. Then it swam around the circle. The huge fish kept its distance . . . but it wasn't going away.

Natalie took control of the boat. She slowly backed it closer to the swimmers. Meanwhile, the dolphin circle was getting smaller and smaller, keeping the swimmers together.

The boat was now at the edge of the circle. "Don't worry," Natalie called. "The dolphins won't let the shark through."

Natalie climbed down to the platform at the back of the boat. "Okay. Swim over to the platform."

The group swam to the boat. Natalie helped Jonathan up first, then Angela. Finally everyone was back on board.

Jonathan whipped off his mask. "That was amazing! Did you see them? Did you see them?"

"Yeah, we were there, remember?" answered Angela. She pulled off her swimming fins and tossed them on the deck. She stood up to see the dolphins swimming away. The shark was swimming away, too, in a different direction.

"Hey, look." Angela pointed to a group of dolphins leaping in the air. A small dolphin was sandwiched between two large ones. "Is that a baby?"

"It sure is," said Natalie. "Its parents are protecting it, just like they protected you."

Angela waved her arm. "Thank you!" she yelled. She didn't know if they heard her or understood. She hoped she would get a chance to thank them again.

CHAPTER 4

A Call for Help

Although their snorkeling trip was cut short, no one was complaining. Jonathan couldn't stop talking about their adventure.

"That was the most awesome thing ever." Dolphins were quickly becoming his favorite animals.

"Have you seen those dolphins before?" Jason asked Natalie.

"Yes. We've been studying that **pod** for years."

"How many dolphins make up a pod?" asked Angela.

"Usually five to ten dolphins. They search for food together and protect one another, especially their young."

---

pod – a group or family of dolphins or whales

"I've read that dolphins often come to people's rescue," said Victor. "There are stories of people being saved from drowning by dolphins pushing them to shore."

"Right," agreed Susan. "And I read about other swimmers being saved from shark attacks just like we were."

Everyone agreed that dolphins are amazing creatures.

Angela and Jonathan discovered that they were playful too. One afternoon, they played catch with Half Moon. Actually, it was more like volleyball. Half Moon would flip the ball out of the water, or jump and smack it with her snout.

Half Moon was a regular visitor to the waters near the research center. Natalie had even taught her a few commands. Half Moon seemed to enjoy the contact with people. Especially with Sid, a young boy about Jonathan's age. Sid visited Half Moon every week. He would have loved to swim with her, but he couldn't. He was in a wheelchair. Half Moon seemed to understand. They had a special friendship.

Sid came by when Angela and Jonathan were playing with Half Moon. They all had a great time. Half Moon came right up to the dock where they were sitting. Then she and Sid "shook hands."

Spending time with Half Moon always made Sid feel better. Maybe it was her gentleness. Maybe it was that built-in smile. Maybe it was the somersaults and volleyball. Whatever it was, Angela and Jonathan understood that dolphins help people in all kinds of ways.

Later that day Angela and Jonathan explored the shore near the research center. The shoreline was mostly sandy beach. But here and there, rocky ground jutted out into the sea. It was a perfect place to look for seashells.

"Oh, here's a pretty one." Angela pulled a half-buried seashell out of the sand. She waded into the water to wash it off. Then she saw something out of the corner of her eye. "Hey, Jon, look!"

Jonathan, who had been watching a sand crab, looked where Angela pointed. A dolphin launched itself high into the air and landed with a splash.

"Cool! Come on, Angie." Jonathan ran toward the dolphin. Angela was quick on his heels.

As they ran, they saw that there were two dolphins close to shore. One kept jumping. The other showed only its head.

Angela and Jonathan walked carefully on the rocks in their flip-flops. When they reached the water, they got another surprise.

"Jon, it's a baby!"

A small dolphin lay in the water near the rocks. Angela expected it to dive when she called out. Instead, it just tilted its head slightly. Angela looked into the gentle eye that stared back. Suddenly she knew that this was the

dolphin family who had helped protect them against the shark.

"Oh no, it's hurt!" A large fishhook was stuck into the baby's side. Fishing line was still attached to the hook. The line wrapped several times around the baby dolphin's tail and one of its flippers. The hook had torn open a wound about three inches long. A small stream of blood trailed from it into the water.

"Jon, go get Mom and Dad. I'll stay here with the dolphin. Hurry!"

CHAPTER 5

A Dangerous Operation

Angela looked again at the wound. The baby must have accidentally been caught by a fisherman. Frightened, the dolphin probably twisted and turned to try and get away. But it became tangled in the line. The parents then led their baby here, close to shore. Close to the research center. They were trying to get help!

"It's okay, little buddy, we'll help you. Just hang in there." Angela knelt on the rocks and held out her hand. The baby inched its way toward her. She gently stroked the baby's nose. Five minutes later Jonathan came running across the beach with Mom, Dad, and Jason. The other scientists were away for the rest of the afternoon. This job was up to Wildlife Rescue.

They quickly sized up the situation. The fishing line was wound so tight that it was cutting into the dolphin's skin. They would have to remove the line first. Then worry about the hook.

"Should we get the ambulance?" asked Victor.

Jason shook his head. "Paul took it for the afternoon. He's doing a training session with a group of volunteers up the coast. We could try our truck, but it might get stuck in this soft sand."

Susan agreed. "We'll have to do this here. I'll go in first."

The water near the rocks was about four feet deep. Susan wasn't sure how the dolphins would react to her. Would they think she was going to harm their baby? Would they attack her? She had to chance it. She slipped into the water.

Susan reached over to the little dolphin and petted it. She could tell the baby was nervous. It was a male. His body trembled beneath her touch. She petted him for a minute until he calmed down. The dolphin parents watched carefully from ten feet away. They seemed to trust her.

Susan looked up. "Okay guys, you're going to have to hold him."

Victor and Jason got in the water. Victor held the tail. Jason took the side opposite Susan.

"Angie, hand me the syringe, please. It's in a small case in my backpack."

Angela took out the syringe and handed it to her mom. Susan gave the baby a shot of medicine to take away some of the pain.

"Okay, now the scissors."

Susan carefully cut the fishing line in several places. She pulled the strands loose one by one. Some strands were embedded deep in the skin. The young dolphin squealed and wiggled when Susan pulled them out. She felt bad hurting him, but she had no choice.

Then something amazing happened. The mother dolphin glided behind Jason and floated near her baby. She gently rubbed its head with her nose. She was comforting her baby.

Everyone smiled. Angela's eyes welled up with tears. It was one of the sweetest things she had ever seen.

Susan noticed it too but stayed focused on her work. "Okay, now comes the hard part. This hook is pretty deep. I want to take it out without causing any more damage. Angela, look in my bag. I need the pliers with the yellow handles and curved ends, please."

This instrument was like a long, thin pair of scissors. Instead of cutting things, it was used to grab things. Susan expertly slid the instrument into the wound and down the length of the hook. She could feel where the point of the hook stuck into the flesh.

The dolphin squealed out in pain. Susan acted quickly. She grabbed the end of the hook and pulled it out of the wound. Done! The baby quickly calmed down.

More blood came out of the wound. Angela gave her mother a clean cloth. Dr. Montoya then pressed the cloth against the wound.

"I'll have to hold this until the bleeding stops," she said. "It should be several minutes."

"Will he be all right?" asked Angela.

"I think so. But I need to stitch this wound. It's too big to let it heal by itself."

"Can you do that here?" asked Victor.

"I'd rather not. It would be better at the research center. Then we could keep an eye on him for a couple days. But we don't have a safe way to get him up there."

"We could try carrying him all the way on the stretcher. He weighs only about 60 pounds."

"Yes, but he's slippery. And if we drop him, he could get hurt more."

While everyone else was talking, Jonathan was looking at the father dolphin. He had stayed about ten or fifteen feet away during the operation. Sometimes he swam back and forth. Jonathan thought he looked like he was guarding the others.

Suddenly the dolphin darted off.

"Where's he going?" asked Jonathan.

Jason shielded his eyes from the late afternoon sun. He looked out across the water. Then he pointed.

"There!"

A large shark fin was slicing through the water and coming right at them. It was about a hundred feet away and closing fast!

CHAPTER 6

A Fond Farewell

"**Q**uick, get out of the water!" There's a shark!" Jonathan yelled.

"We can't leave the baby here," Susan replied. "Anyway, we're fine. The parent dolphins will fight off the shark."

She was right. The father took off after the shark with lightning speed. He rammed his strong snout into the shark's soft underbelly. Wildlife Rescue could tell what was happening because they saw the shark's fin suddenly jerk to the side.

Still, the shark kept coming.

"It must smell the baby dolphin's blood in the water," said Victor. "Sharks have an incredible sense of smell."

Suddenly the mother bolted toward the shark as well. A few seconds later, its fin once again jerked to the side. Then again . . . and again. Both dolphins were pounding the huge hungry fish. Finally, after 30 long seconds, the shark turned and swam away. It would have to look for food elsewhere.

Angela and Jonathan applauded from the shore.

"Dolphins 1, shark 0," announced Angela.

"That'll teach that mean ol' shark," said Jonathan.

Jason calmly corrected him. "The shark isn't mean, Jon. It's just hungry. It's one of the ocean's most skilled **predators.** If it smells blood, it knows that a dead or injured animal is in the area. That usually means an easy meal."

"Yeah, well, not this time," replied Jonathan.

Jason agreed, and smiled.

At that moment the parent dolphins burst from the water head over tail in a somersault.

"Looks like a victory celebration," laughed Victor.

The dolphins then swam back to their baby and Wildlife Rescue. Jason petted the mother as everyone said thank you for the second time that week.

"Hey, what's that?" Angela noticed an all-terrain vehicle racing toward them across the beach. It was a small, light vehicle with wide tires. So it didn't get stuck in the sand.

As the vehicle approached, they could see that it was Natalie and Paul.

---

predator – an animal that hunts other animals for food

"Boy, are we glad to see you," said Susan.

Paul hopped out. "We just got back and saw the note you left on the door. What's going on?"

Susan explained what had happened. Jonathan chimed in with a few details about the hook and the blood and the shark attack.

"That's Ozzie and Harriet," Paul said pointing to the parent dolphins, "and their son Ricky."

He agreed with Susan that it would be best to take Ricky back to the research center. "We brought a stretcher. We can strap him across the back of the ATV. I'll drive slowly while the rest of you walk alongside. You can make sure he doesn't fall off."

Natalie handed four buckets to Angela and Jonathan. "Fill these buckets with water. We'll use them to sponge down Ricky on the way."

It was a struggle getting Ricky on the stretcher, but they managed. The parent dolphins made loud creaking noises when they saw what was happening.

"Ozzie and Harriet aren't too happy about this," noted Paul.

"They're not stopping us, though," said Jason. "I think they know we're still helping their baby."

Angela was curious about the names. "Why did you call them Ozzie and Harriet?"

Natalie laughed. "It's from an old TV show. Ricky was the son, and Ozzie and Harriet were the perfect parents. Just like our dolphins."

Paul and Susan stitched Ricky's wound. Soon the cuts from the fishing line began to heal. It was clear, though, that the baby missed his parents and the other dolphins in the pod.

The scientists decided to release Ricky after two days. They took him to the same spot where they found him. Ozzie and Harriet had stayed in the area. That was a relief to Angela. She was afraid that Ricky would not be able to find his parents again.

"It wouldn't matter too much, though, even if his parents were not still here," her dad assured her. "When a dolphin is born, the mother and baby whistle to each other. The whistle is one of a kind. That way, the dolphins can find each other if they get lost or separated."

Wildlife Rescue and several people from the research center gathered to see Ricky off. His parents met him about 50 feet from the shore. They swam around each other. They leaped in the air. Then they headed out to sea.

Everyone waved. "Thanks Ozzie! Thanks Harriet! Bye Ricky!" Angela got to thank them again after all.

The Facts Behind the Story

Bottlenose Dolphins

Dolphins grow to be up to 12 feet long. Their sleek bodies are usually gray on top with whitish undersides. A bottlenose dolphin's snout is long, and lined with sharp teeth. Dolphins are mammals and breathe air through blowholes on the tops of their heads. They are also fast and powerful swimmers. Dolphins live along coasts in groups called pods.

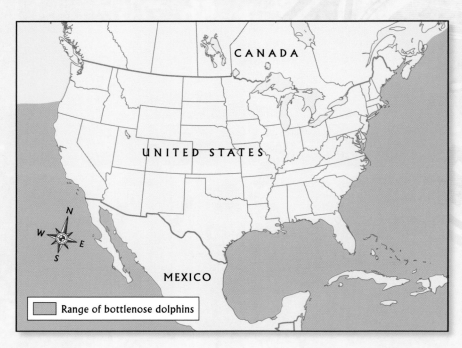

Range of bottlenose dolphins

What Dolphins Eat

Dolphins hunt by chasing down their food. They use
their sharp teeth to catch and hold on to fish, eels, and
slippery squid. Their strong jaws crunch through the
shells of crabs. When it is hard to see in the water, a
dolphin has a special way of finding food. It sends out
a clicking sound. The sound waves hit an object like
a fish and bounce back in an echo. The echo tells the
dolphin where to find the fish. Sometimes dolphins
work together to herd fish. This makes the fish easier
to catch.

Baby Dolphins

Dolphins have babies in the spring or summer. A baby dolphin is about three feet long and begins swimming as soon as it is born. A helper or "auntie" dolphin in the pod helps the mother push the baby to the surface to get its first breath of air. The auntie stays with mother and baby and helps protect the baby dolphin from sharks. The baby drinks milk from its mother. After a few months it will start eating fish. Young dolphins stay close to their mothers for three years.

Write A Class Report

Think about what you have learned about bottlenose dolphins. Imagine that you are a guide taking people on a dolphin-watching tour. What questions do you think people on the tour will have? What answers will you give them?

- Copy the chart below.
- In one column write some questions about bottlenose dolphins. In the other column write the answers.

Questions	Answers
How big do dolphins grow?	Dolphins can grow to be about 12 feet long.

Read More About Dolphins

Find and read more books about dolphins. As you read, think about these questions. They will help you understand more about this topic.

- Are there other types of dolphins? How are they different from the bottlenose dolphin?

- Do other animals use echoes to find food?

- Can scientists understand dolphin "talk"?

- Do dolphins stay with a pod for their whole lives?

SUGGESTED READING
Reading Expeditions
Life Science:
Animal Adaptations